HOW TO DRAW
ALL THE ANIMALS
for kids

ALLI KOCH

Written and illustrated by Alli Koch

ISBN:
9781950968237

Printed in Colombia
10 9 8 7 6 5

this book

BELONGS TO

_____

JUNGLE
8

SAFARI
16

SEA
24

DOWN UNDER
32

FARM
40

FOREST
48

ARCTIC
56

PETS
64

INSECTS
72

LET'S DRAW!

The nice thing about being an artist is that you can make the rules. Everyone has their own style, which is why your drawings will look different from someone else's. In this book, each animal is broken down into steps. My goal is to help you see the simple parts of what may seem like a hard thing to draw.

We will start with the most basic outline or guide and work our way up. You will start to see a pattern with each animal we draw; starting with simple guide lines, then breaking down "C" and "S" shape lines, and lastly erasing the unneeded lines for the finished look. Don't forget to draw your lines lightly first so it is easier to erase them. My favorite thing to say when drawing is:

If it was perfect, it would not look handmade!

I cannot wait for you to get started. Happy drawing!

TOOLS

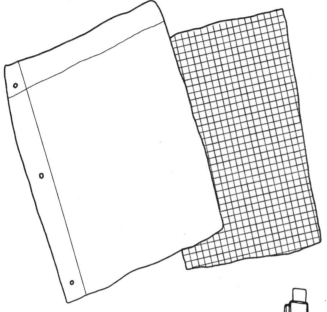

The cool thing about art is that you can use any tool you want! Yep, that's right! You are the artist, so feel free to be creative. For this book, let's keep it simple. It's easy to learn using either blank sheets of paper or grid paper.

When you are learning to draw, you really only need a pencil and a good eraser. To follow the step-by-step instructions: draw everything lightly, then go over your lines with whichever tool you would like to use. You can use different pens, markers, colored pencils, or even crayons to add details to your animals.

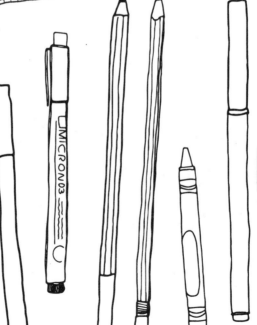

CIRCLES CAN BE TRICKY. TRY USING A PENNY OR A CIRCLE STENCIL TO HELP!

BREAK IT DOWN

Anyone can draw! If you can write your ABCs (which I am pretty sure that you can!), then you can draw everything in this book. Each animal can be broken down into a bunch of "C" and "S" shaped lines. Almost anything that is round is two simple "C" lines put together. An "S" line is for when something has a dip or curvy line.

All of the animals in this book are broken down into six steps. What you will draw in each step will be a black line; what you have already done will be in gray line. There are 56 animals total in this book for you to learn how to draw. The chapter dividers in this book are also bonus coloring pages that you can color!

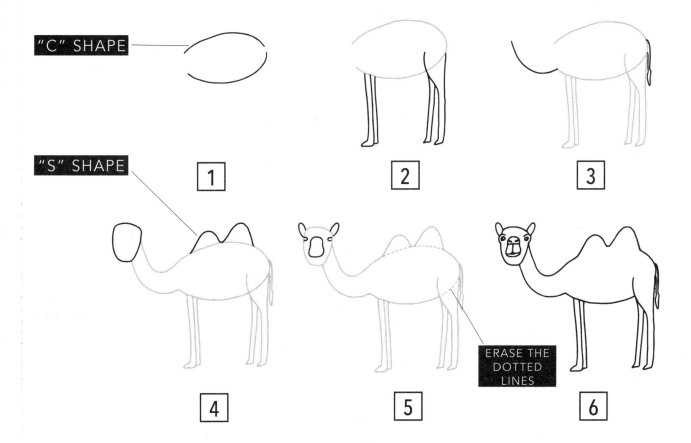

"C" SHAPE

"S" SHAPE

1

2

3

4

5
ERASE THE DOTTED LINES

6

JUNGLE

FROG

You can hypnotize a frog on its back by rubbing its stomach.

1

2

3

4

5

6

MONKEY

A group of monkeys is called a troop or a barrel.

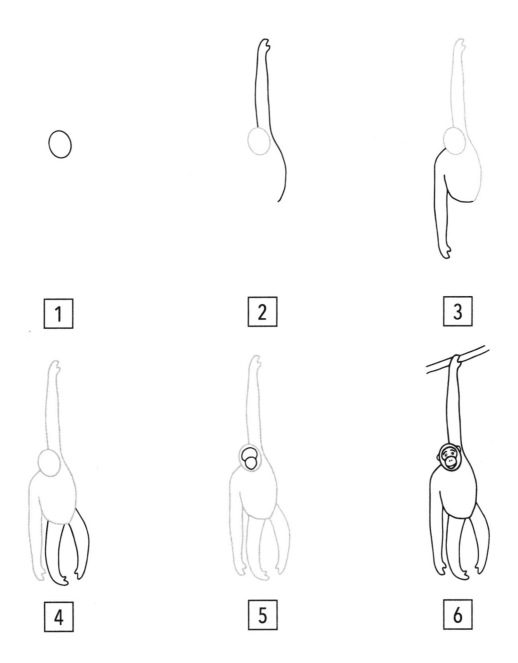

SLOTH

Sloths take two weeks to digest their food.

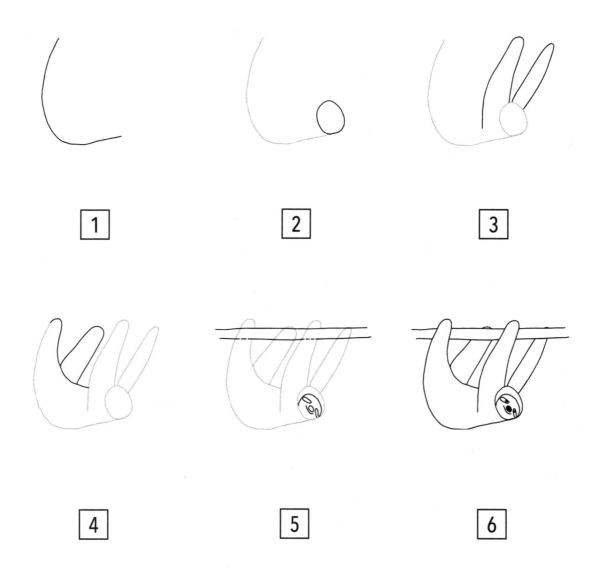

TIGER

Tigers are nocturnal and do most of their hunting at night.

ALLIGATOR

An alligator can go through over 2,000 teeth in its lifetime.

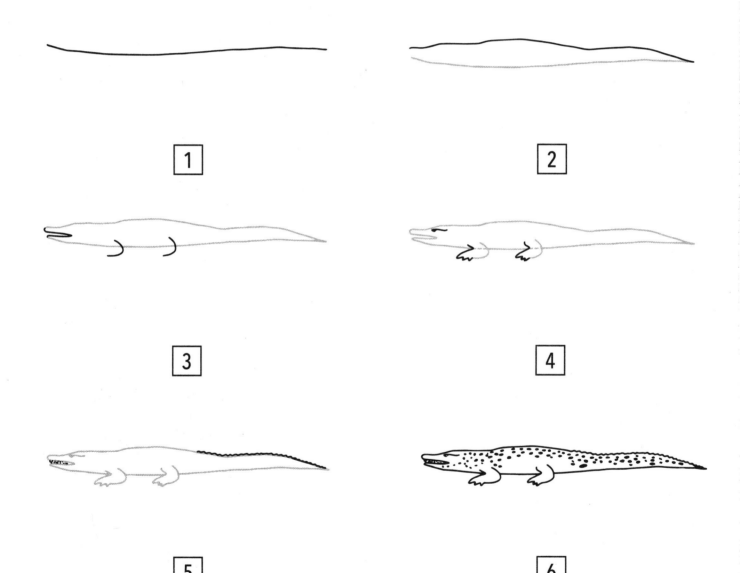

TOUCAN

Toucans are actually close relatives of the woodpecker.

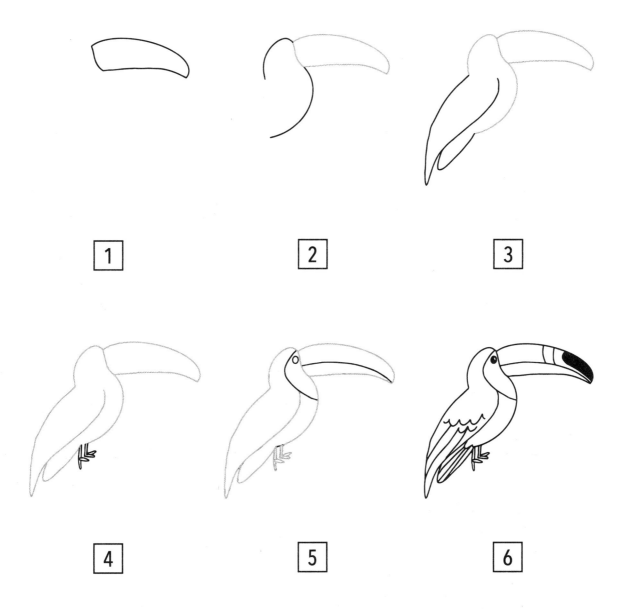

1

2

3

4

5

6

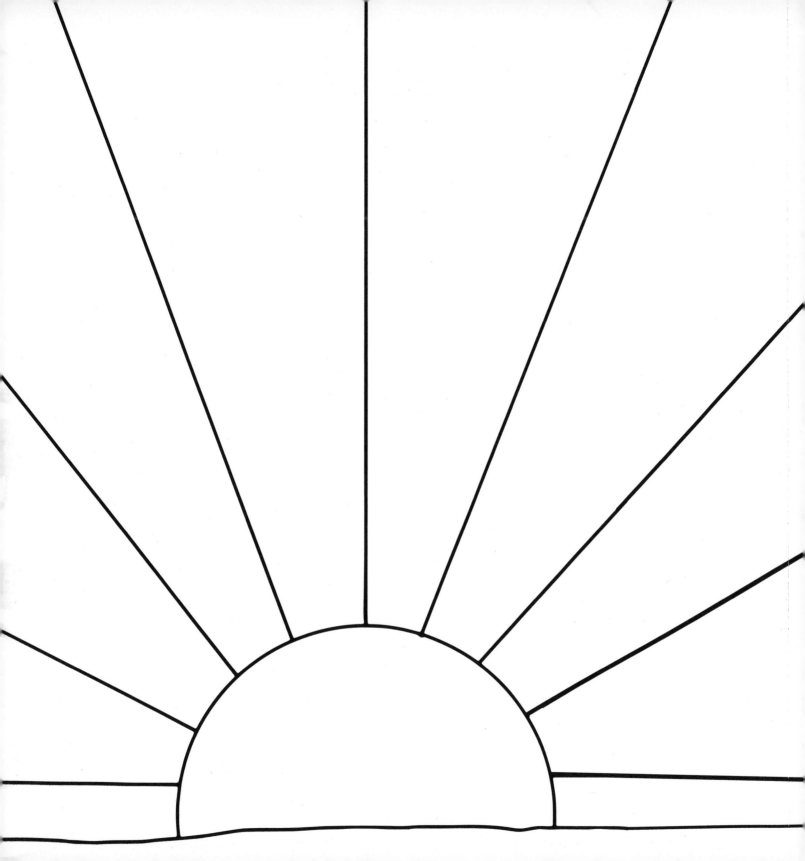

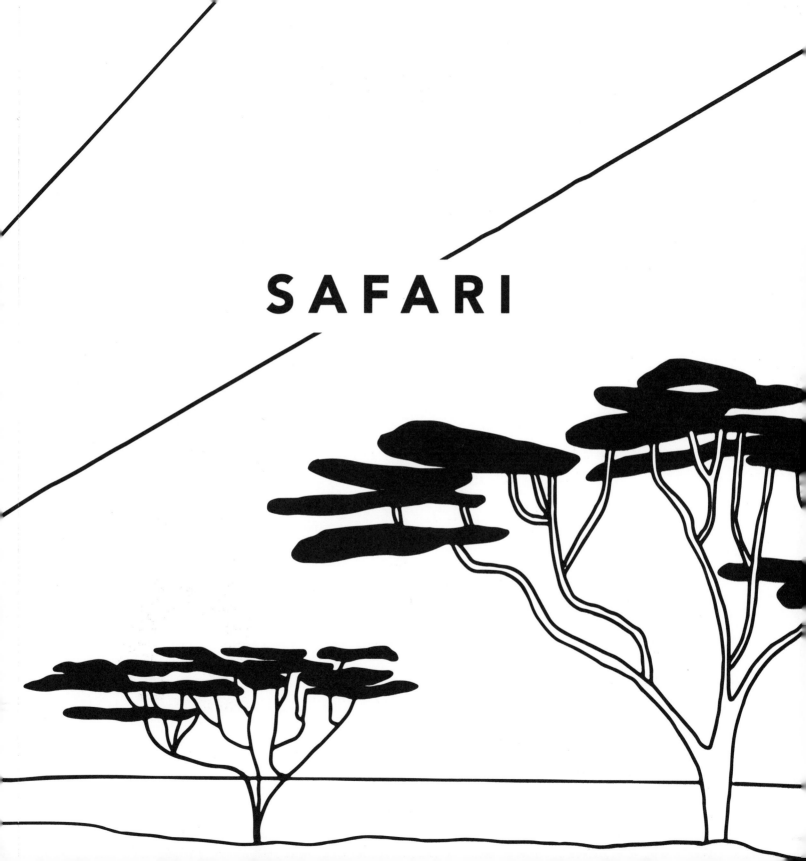

PANDA

Pandas have six fingers. They have an extra thumb that helps them grab bamboo better.

GIRAFFE

A giraffe's tongue can grow to be up to 20 inches long.

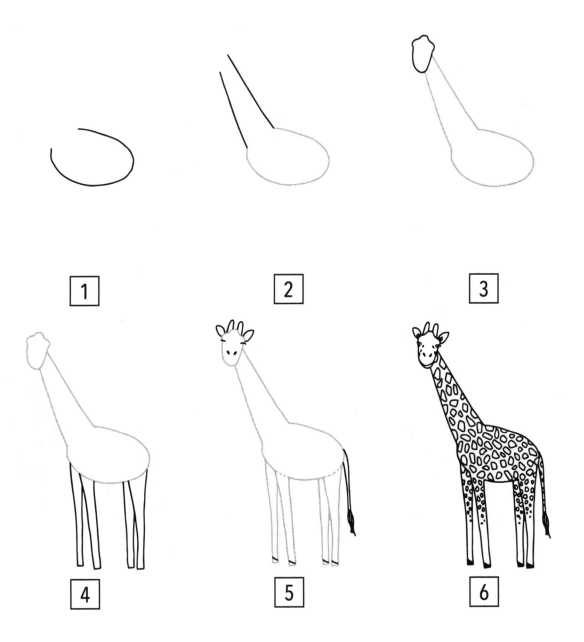

1

2

3

4

5

6

LION

A lion's roar can be heard as far as five miles away.

1

2

3

4

5

6

ELEPHANT

Elephants are too heavy jump.

1

2

3

4

5

6

FLAMINGO

Flamingos are born with gray and white feathers. They turn pink when they turn 1-2 years old.

ZEBRA

Each individual stripe on a zebra is unique and different from the others.

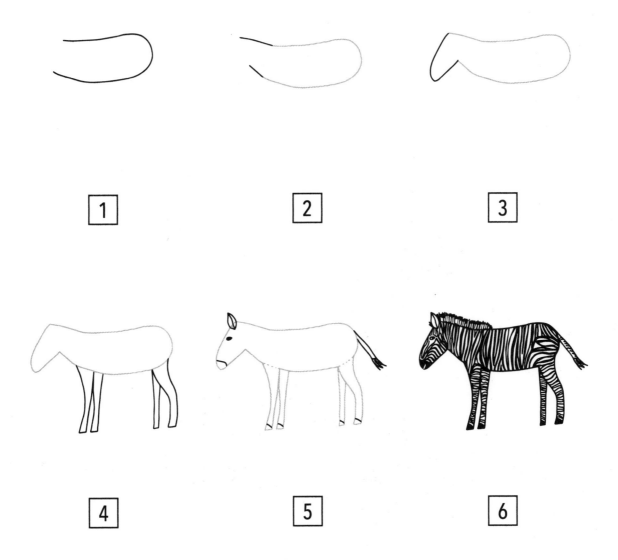

1

2

3

4

5

6

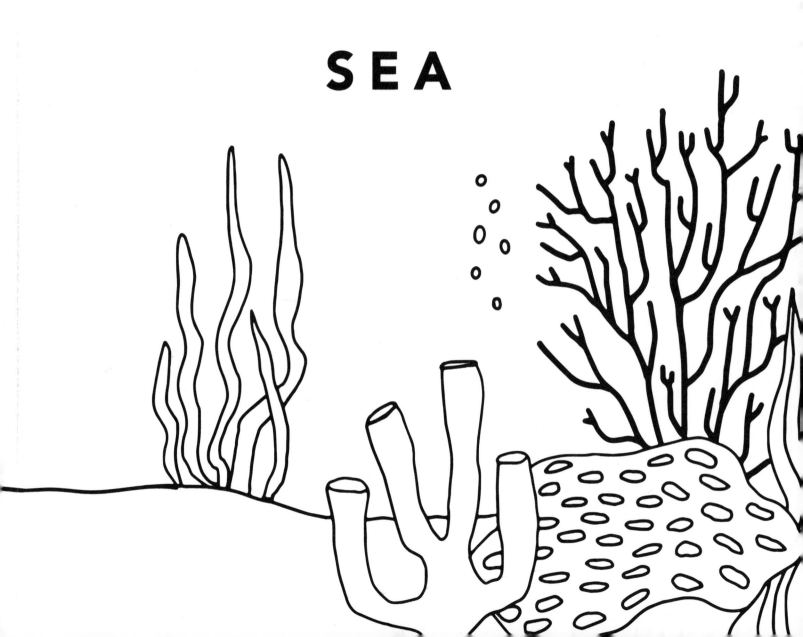

SEA

FISH

There are at least 30,000 different species of fish.

$\boxed{1}$

$\boxed{2}$

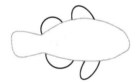

$\boxed{3}$

$\boxed{4}$

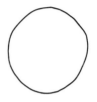

$\boxed{1}$

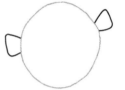

$\boxed{2}$

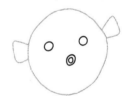

$\boxed{3}$

$\boxed{4}$

SHARK

A shark's skin feels exactly like sandpaper.

1
    2
    3

4
    5
    6

WHALE

Orcas can be found in every ocean.

TURTLE

Leatherback sea turtles have existed since the age of dinosaurs!

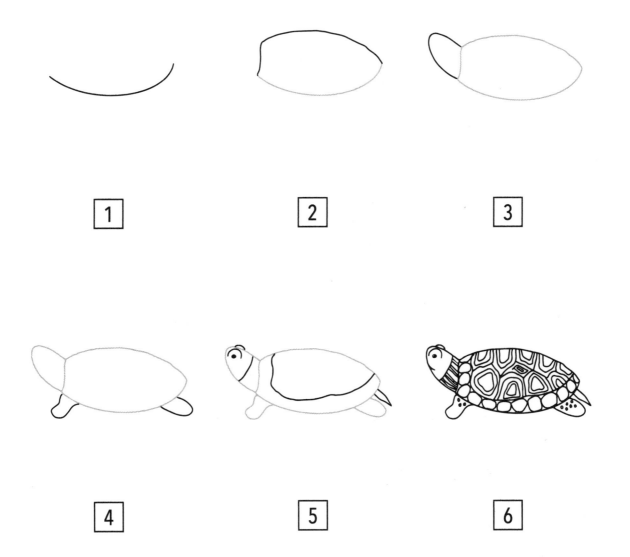

1

2

3

4

5

6

OCTOPUS

An octopus has three hearts.

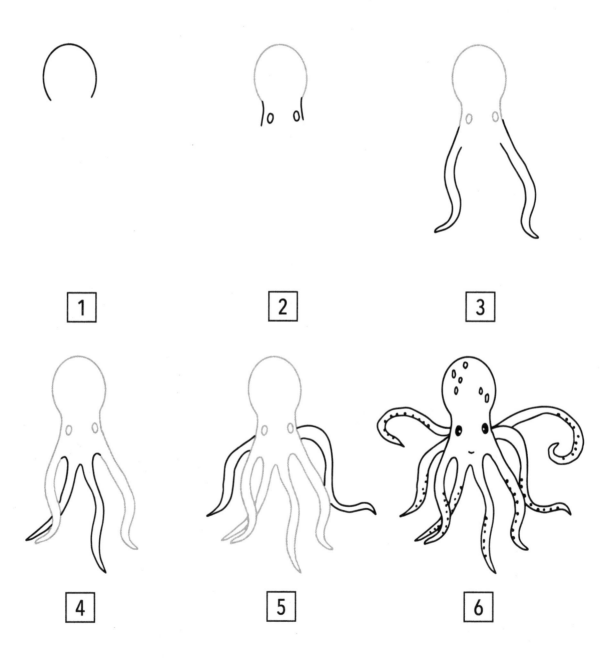

1

2

3

4

5

6

DOLPHIN

Wild dolphins call each other by name.

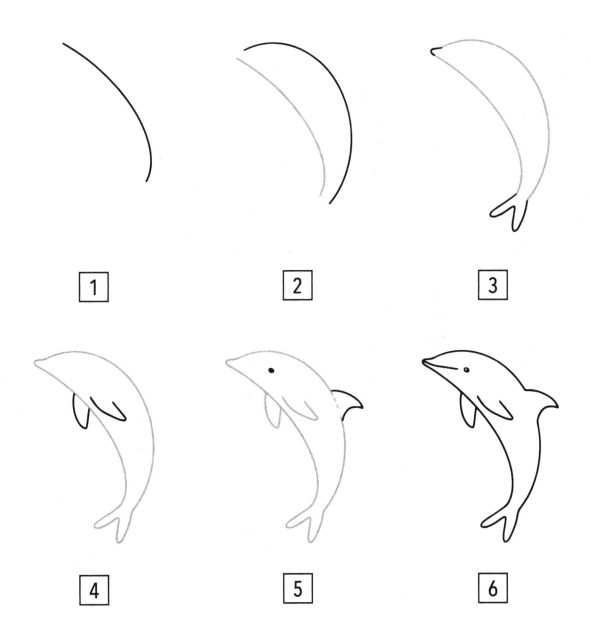

DOWN
UNDER

KOALA

Koala bears have fingerprints just like human fingerprints.

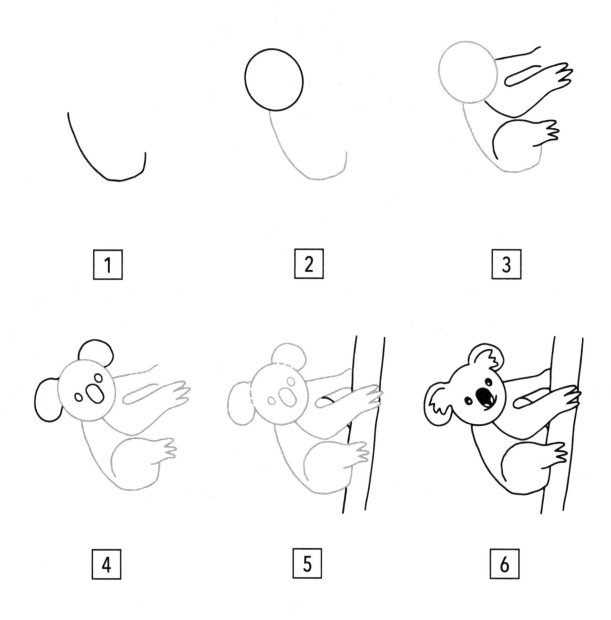

KANGAROO

A baby kangaroo is called a joey.

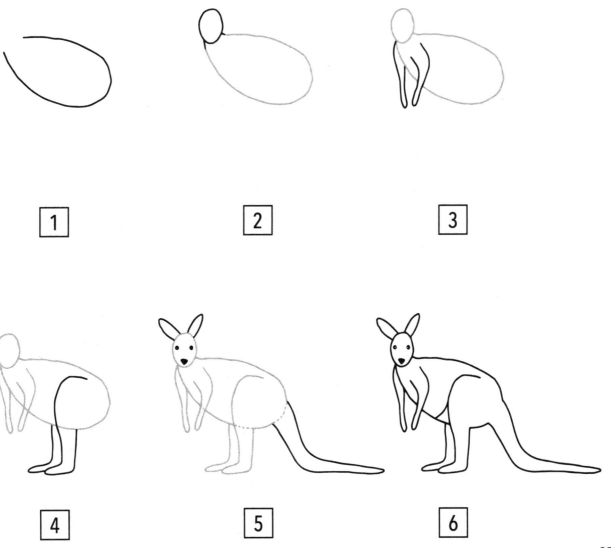

1

2

3

4

5

6

EMU

Emus are the only bird with calf muscles.

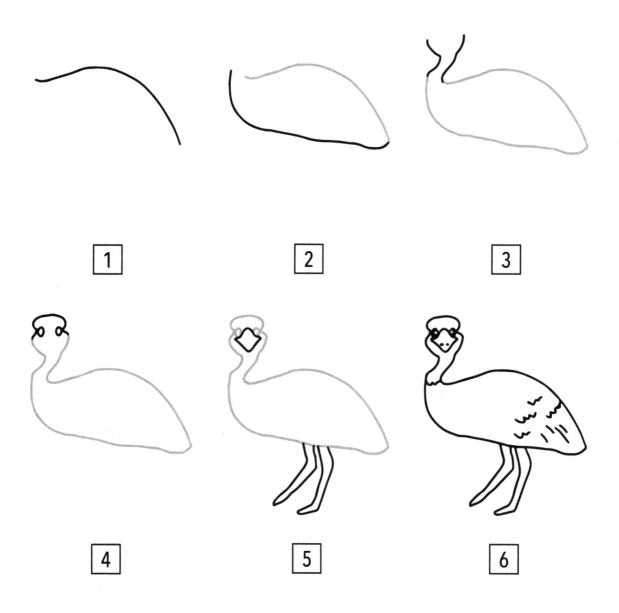

1

2

3

4

5

6

LIZARD

Most baby lizards are able to walk, run, and feed themselves from the time they are born.

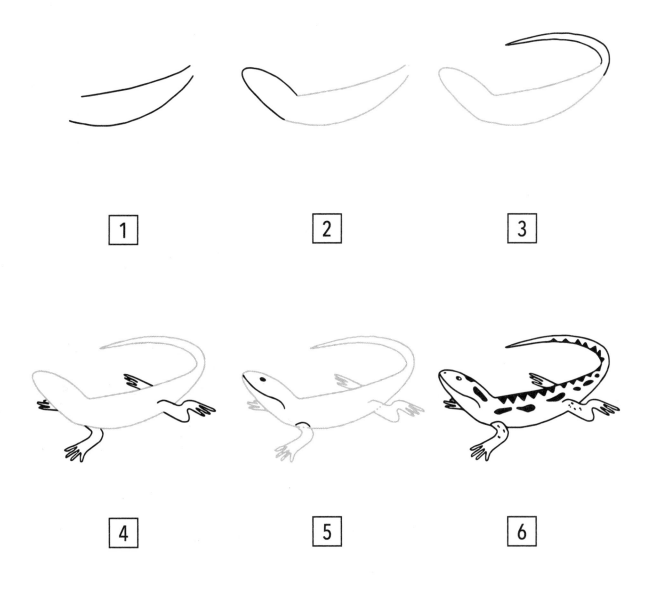

DINGO

Australia has so many dingoes that they built a 3,488-mile fence to keep them contained.

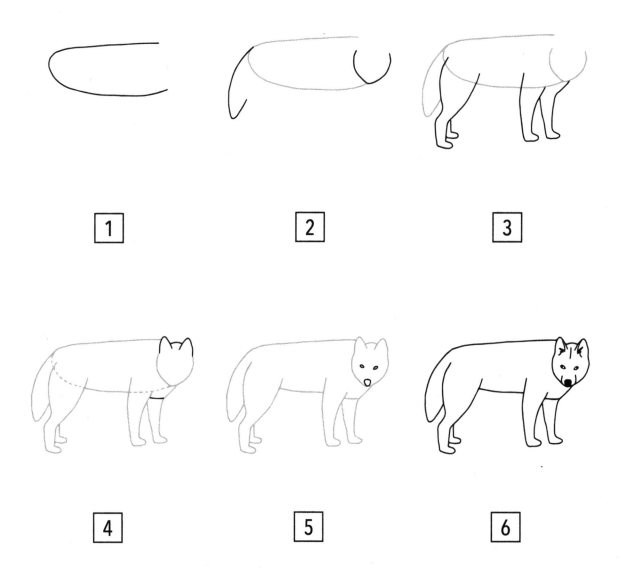

1

2

3

4

5

6

EAGLE

The wedge-tailed eagle is native to Australia and is one of the world's largest eagles.

FARM

COW

Cows are very social animals and love having lots of friends.

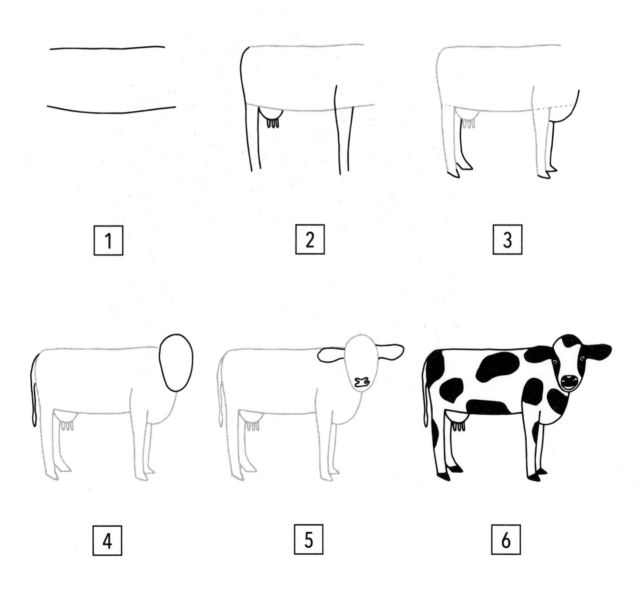

LLAMA

Llamas spit when they are angry or annoyed.

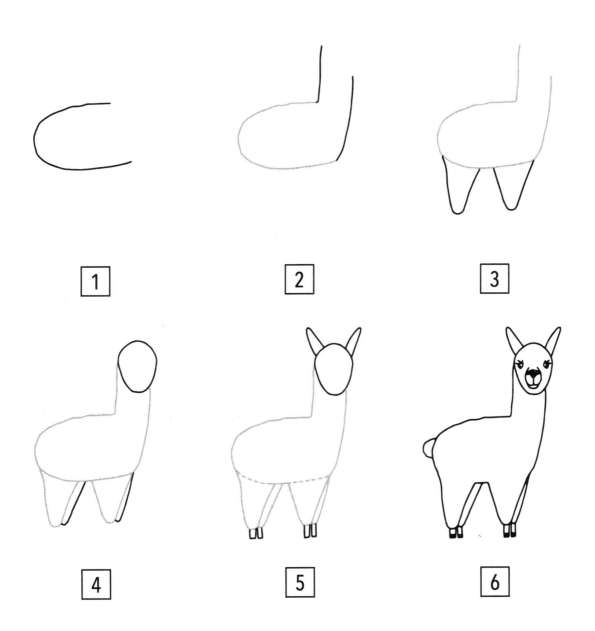

1

2

3

4

5

6

LAMB

A lamb's wool will grow all of its life.

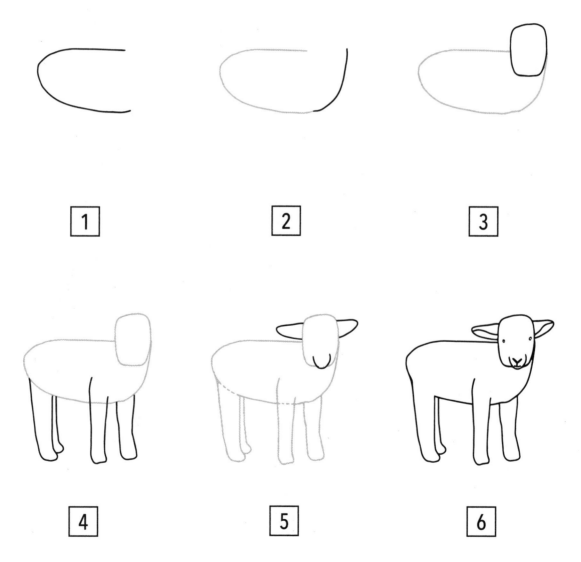

HORSE

A horse's eyeballs are bigger than those of any other land animal.

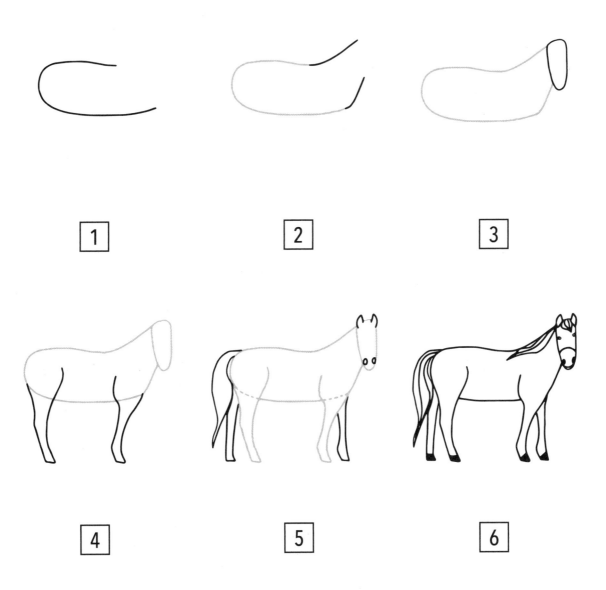

1

2

3

4

5

6

PIG

Pigs are smart and emotional animals. They can even anticipate positive and negative events.

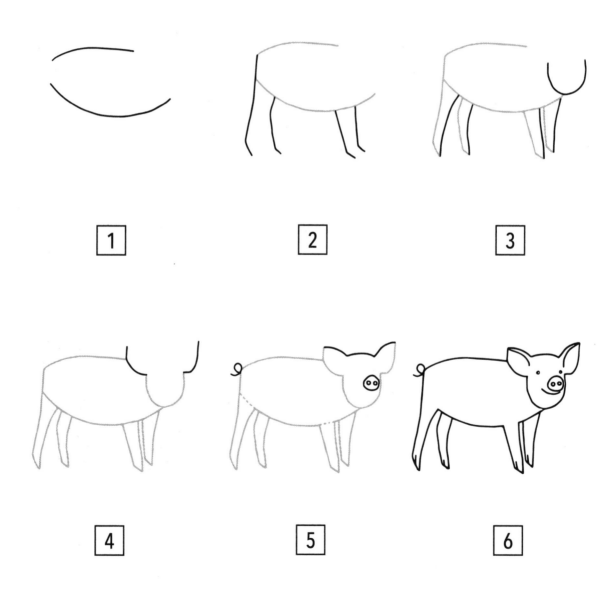

CHICKEN

Chickens can dream while they're sleeping.

1

2

3

4

5

6

FOREST

BEAR

Brown bears actually come in many shades of color, from a light cream to a dark black.

SQUIRREL

Squirrels twitch their tails to signal danger to other squirrels.

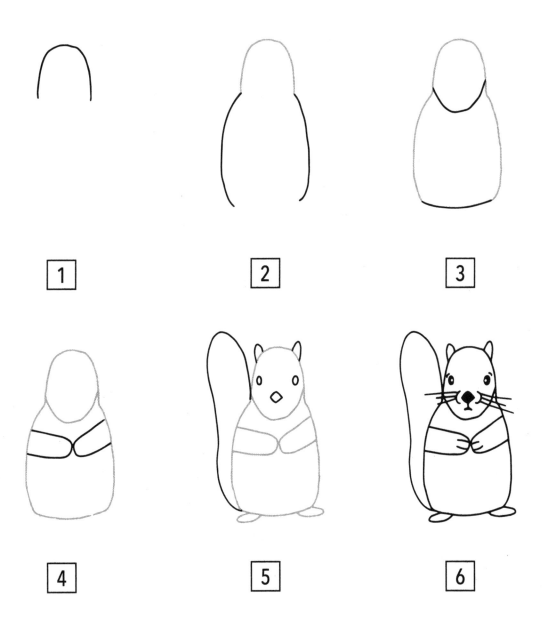

1

2

3

4

5

6

OTTER

Approximately 90 percent of the world's sea otters live in Alaska.

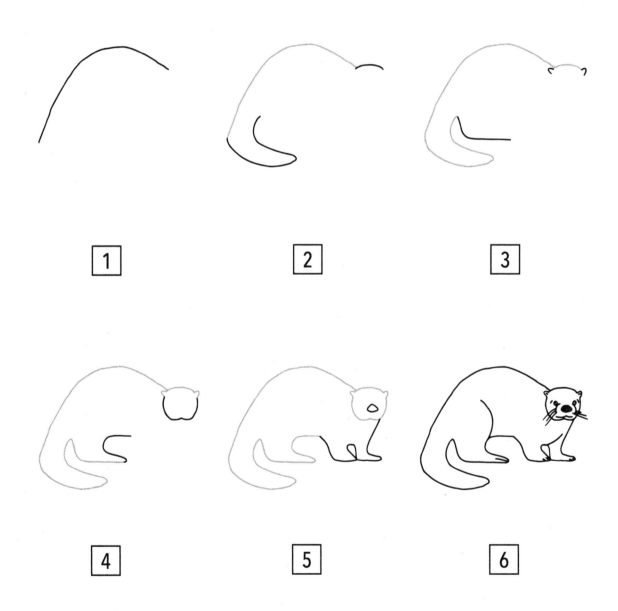

BUNNY

Rabbits' eyes are on the side of their head. They can see almost all the way around them.

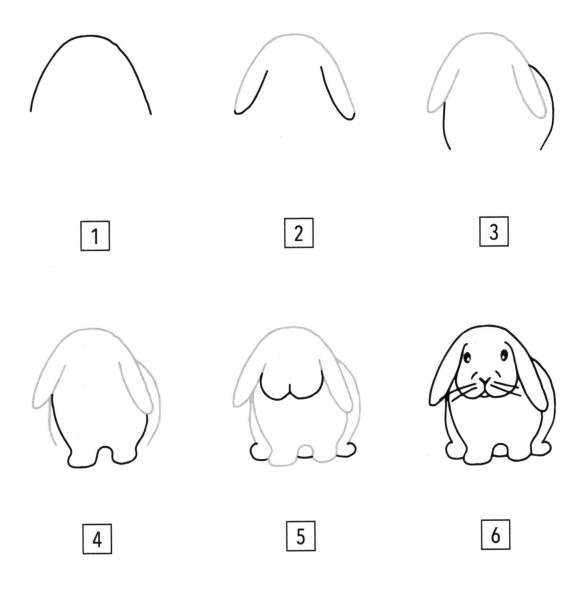

1

2

3

4

5

6

OWL

Owls don't have eyeballs. They have eye tubes.

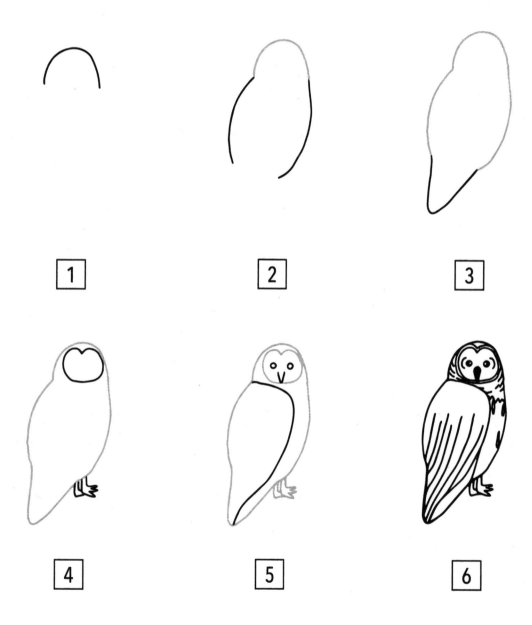

1

2

3

4

5

6

FOX

A female fox is called a "vixen" and a male fox is called a "dog fox" or a "tod."

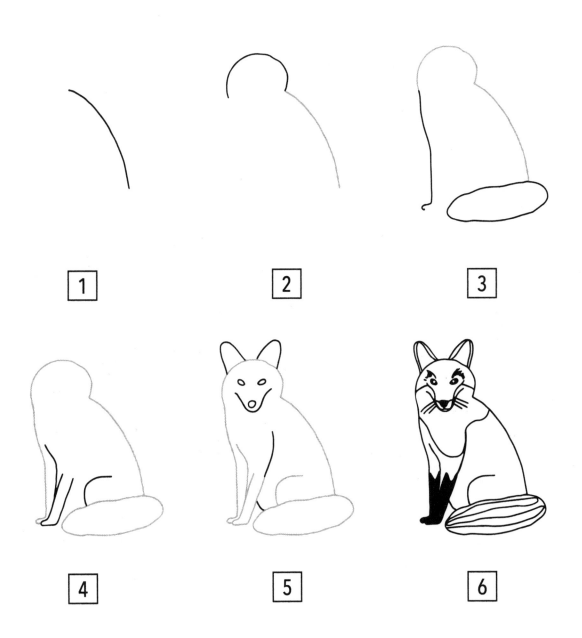

ARCTIC

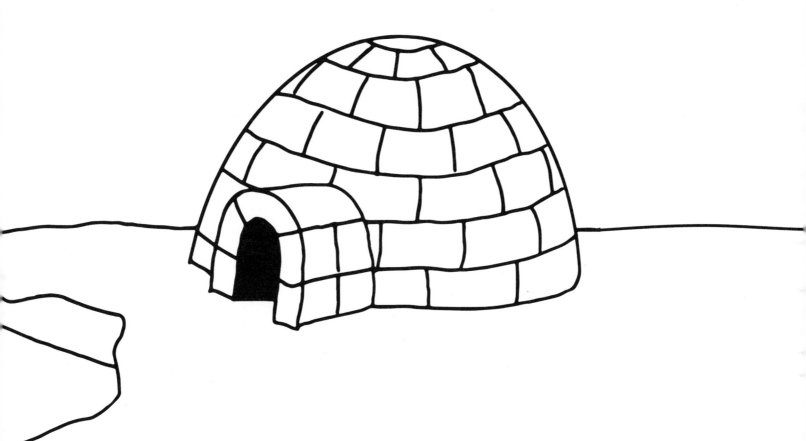

NARWHAL

With a large tusk on their heads, narwhals are considered the unicorns of the sea.

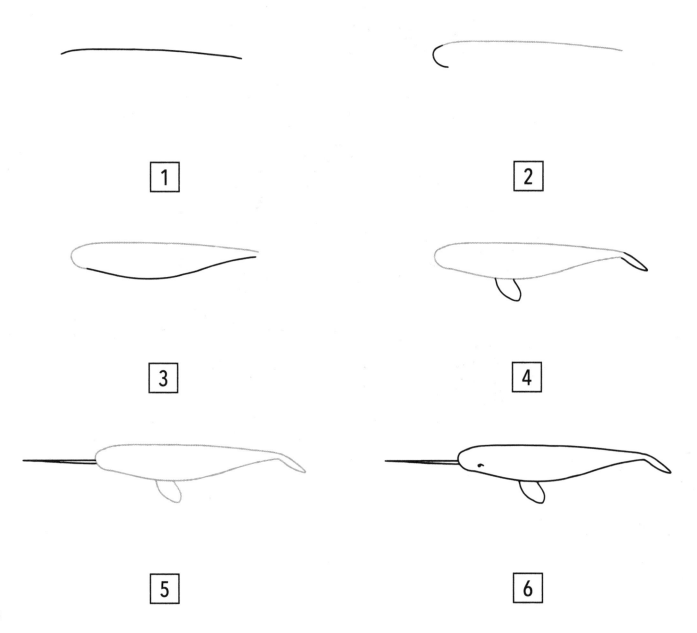

POLAR BEAR

Polar bears can swim for days at a time.

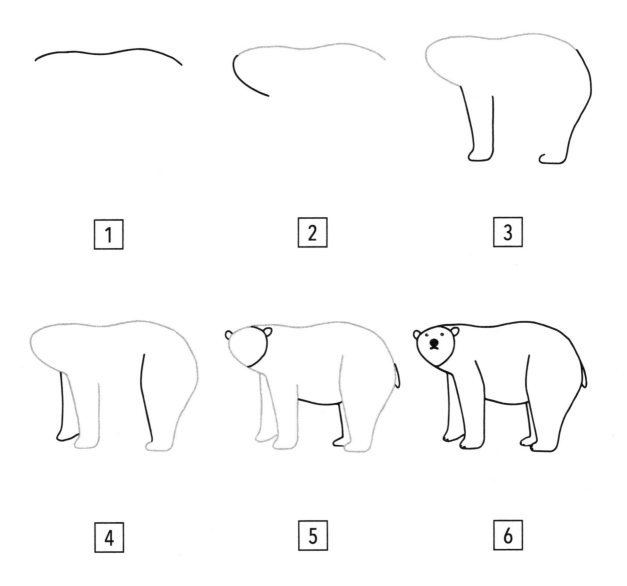

1

2

3

4

5

6

MOOSE

Moose have huge appetites. They can eat up to 73 pounds of food in the summer.

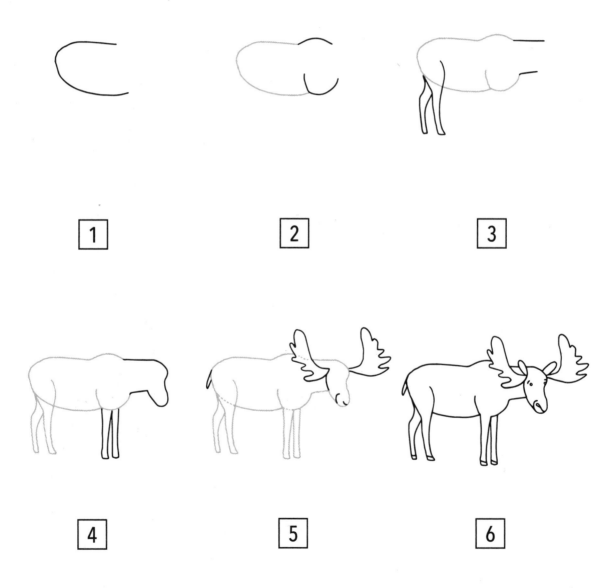

60

SEAL

Seals don't drink sea water. They get all the water they need from their food.

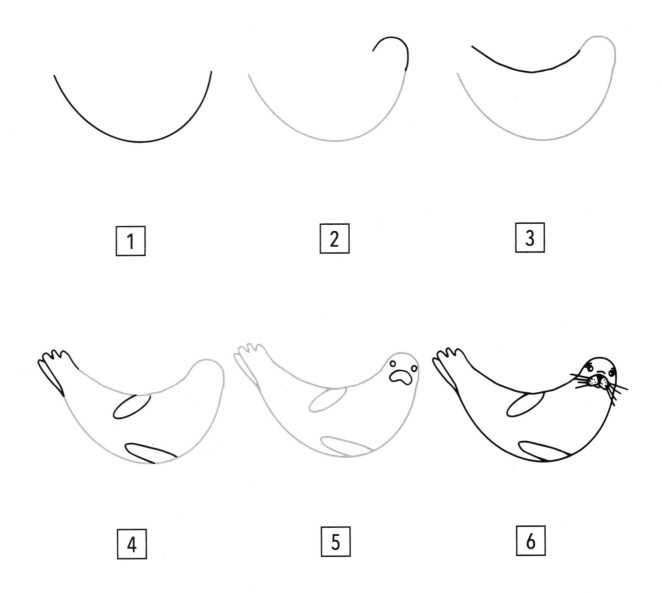

1

2

3

4

5

6

WALRUS

Walruses can nap anywhere, including while floating on water.

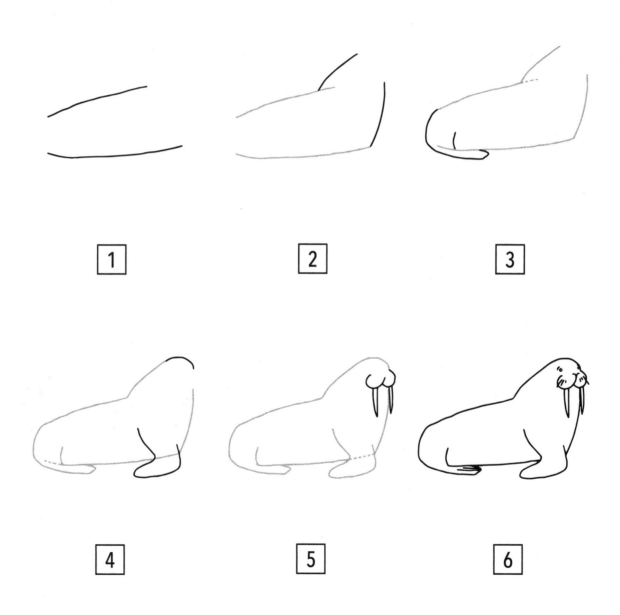

PENGUIN

The black and white "tuxedo" of a penguin is their camouflage. It's called countershading.

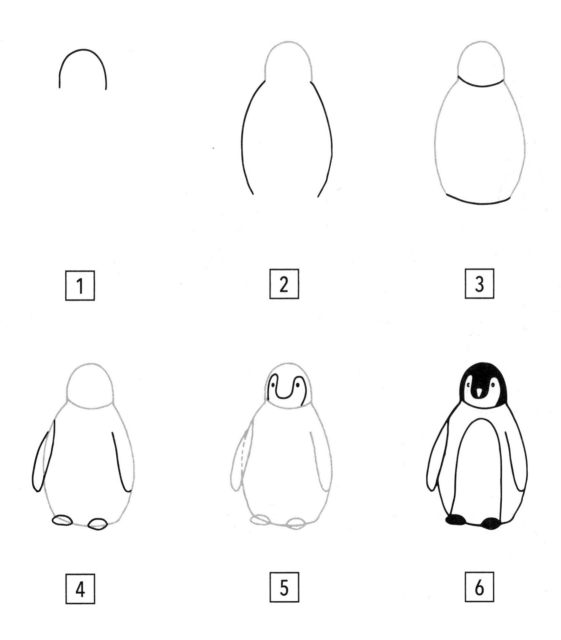

CAT

Cats developed their meows so they could better communicate with humans.

DOG

A dog's sense of smell is 100,000 times more powerful than a human's.

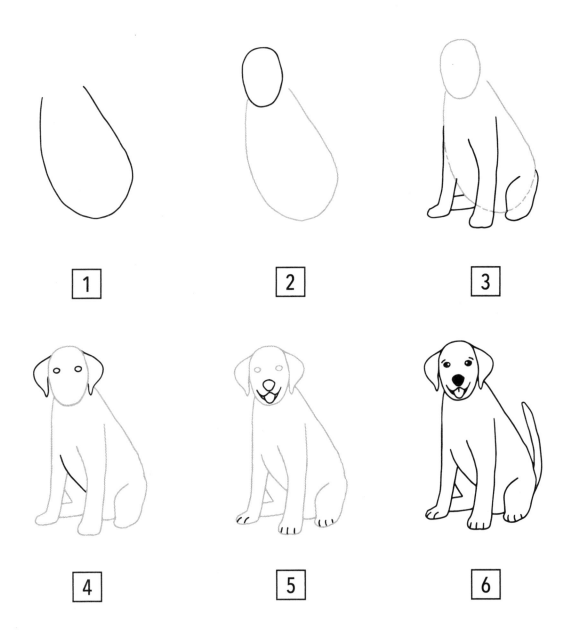

HAMSTER

Hamsters can only see a few inches in front of their noses.

1

2

3

4

5

6

SNAKE

If a snake's head is oval shape, then it is a non-venomous snake.

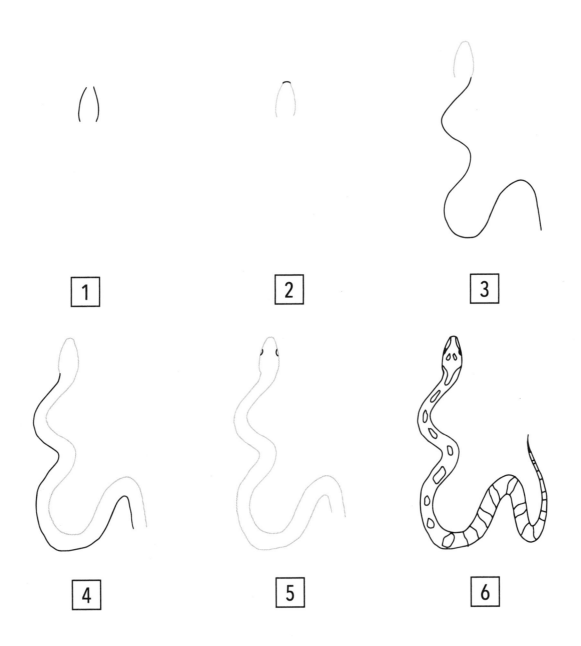

FERRET

Groups of ferrets are called a business.

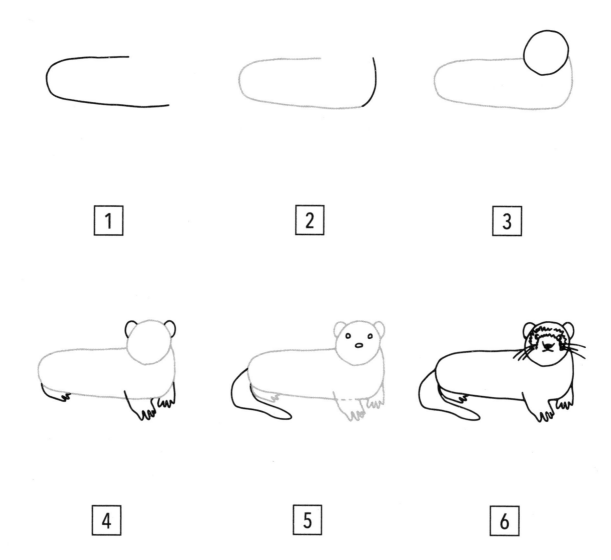

MOUSE

A mouse will play dead if it is really scared of something.

INSECTS

LADYBUG

Depending on the type of ladybug, some species have spots, stripes, or are a solid color.

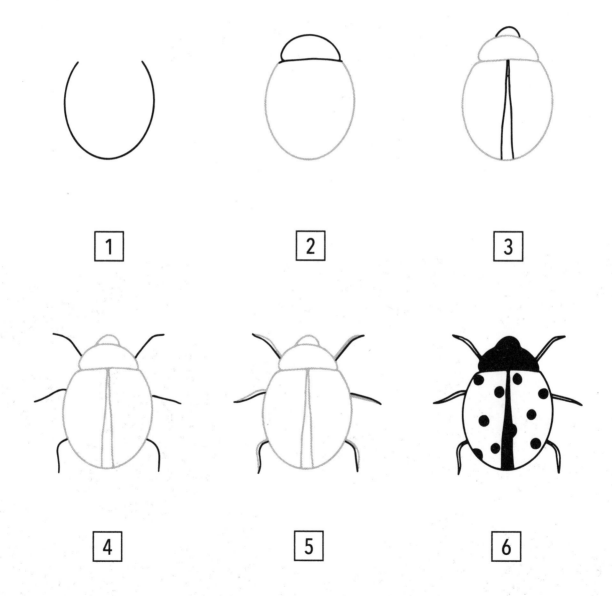

BUTTERFLY

Butterflies can taste with their feet.

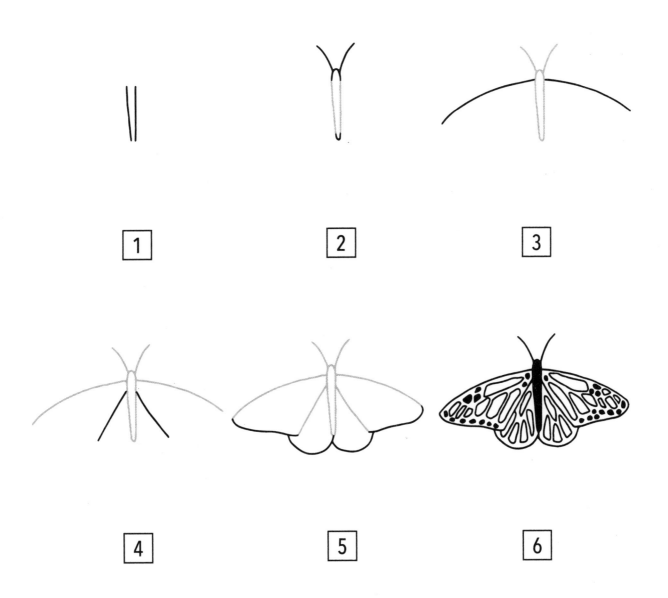

1

2

3

4

5

6

GRASSHOPPER

A grasshopper's back legs act as catapults. They help it jump as far as 30 inches.

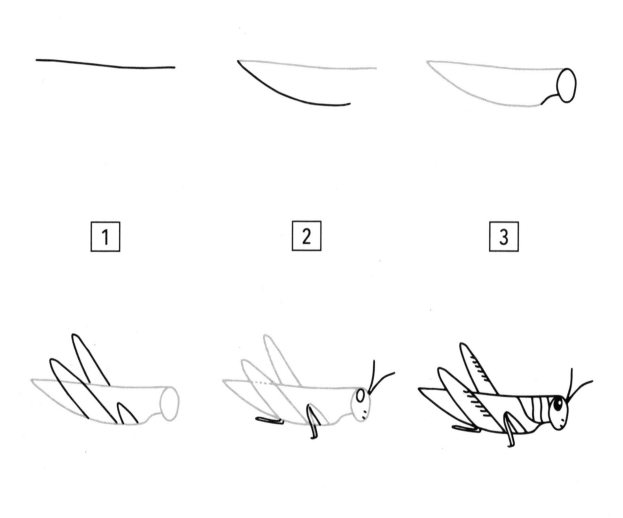

1

2

3

4

5

6

DRAGONFLY

Dragonflies have been around for over 300 million years.

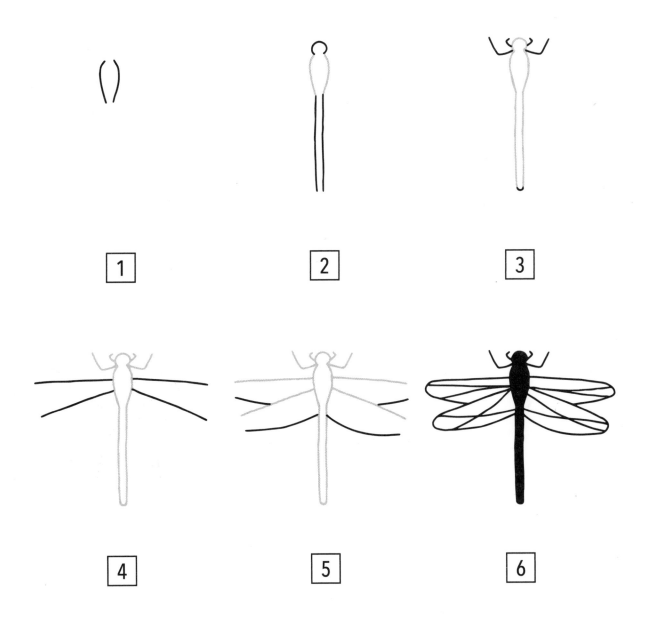

SPIDER

A single strand of spider web is five times stronger than steel of the same width.

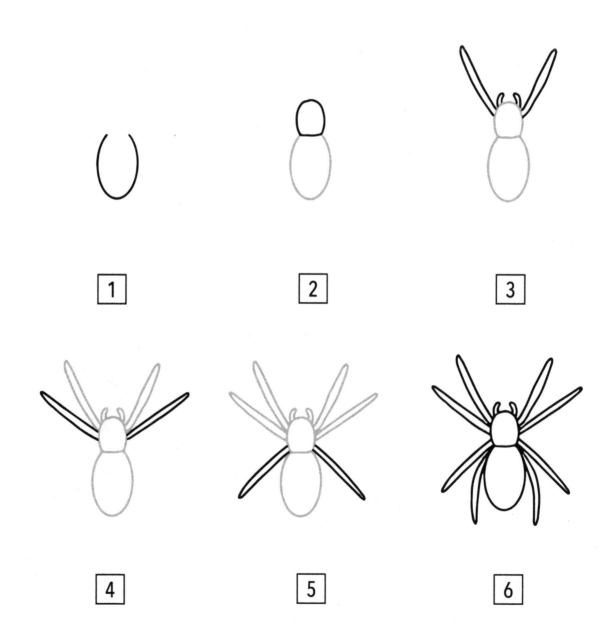

1

2

3

4

5

6

BEE

Honeybees can flap their wings 200 times per second.

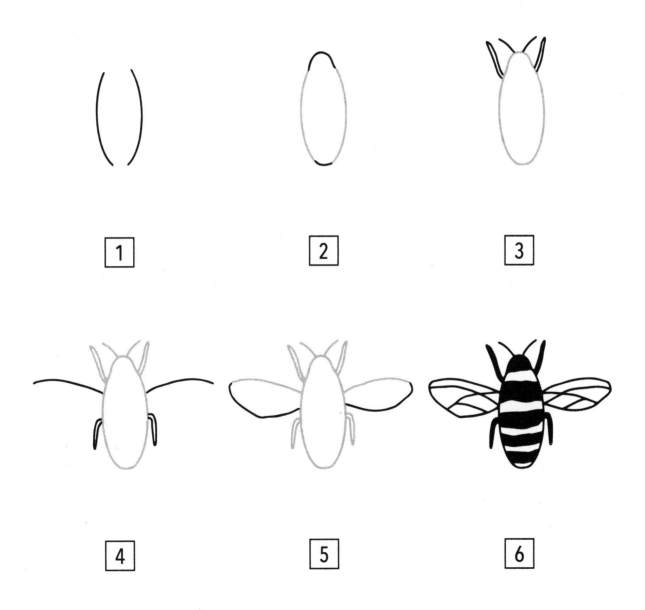

About Alli K

NAME: Alli Koch

HOME: Dallas, Texas

BIRTHDAY: March 20, 1991

FAVORITE COLOR: Black

FAVORITE FOOD: Waffle fries and a large sweet tea

JOB: I am a full-time artist! I sell my art online, paint on the side of buildings, and teach others how to draw or be creative

FAVORITE THING: My planner or blanket

PETS: I have two cats, Emmie and Cleo

CAR: Jeep

FAMILY: Married to my high school sweetheart

FAVORITE ANIMAL: Cats and dolphins

FAVORITE TO DO: Hang outside on a sunny day and eat lunch with friends